ALL AROUND THE WORLD
EL SALVADOR

by Joanne Mattern

pogo

Ideas for Parents and Teachers

Pogo Books let children practice reading informational text while introducing them to nonfiction features such as headings, labels, sidebars, maps, and diagrams, as well as a table of contents, glossary, and index.

Carefully leveled text with a strong photo match offers early fluent readers the support they need to succeed.

Before Reading

- "Walk" through the book and point out the various nonfiction features. Ask the student what purpose each feature serves.

- Look at the glossary together. Read and discuss the words.

Read the Book

- Have the child read the book independently.

- Invite him or her to list questions that arise from reading.

After Reading

- Discuss the child's questions. Talk about how he or she might find answers to those questions.

- Prompt the child to think more. Ask: Did you know about cloud forests before you read this book? What more would you like to know about them?

Pogo Books are published by Jump!
5357 Penn Avenue South
Minneapolis, MN 55419
www.jumplibrary.com

Library of Congress Cataloging-in-Publication Data

Names: Mattern, Joanne, 1963- author.
Title: El Salvador / by Joanne Mattern.
Description: Pogo books. | Minneapolis : Jump!, Inc., [2019]
Series: All around the world | Includes index.
Audience: Ages 7-10.
Identifiers: LCCN 2018018387 (print)
LCCN 2018019039 (ebook)
ISBN 9781641281515 (ebook)
ISBN 9781641281492 (hardcover : alk. paper)
ISBN 9781641281508 (pbk.)
Subjects: LCSH: El Salvador–Juvenile literature.
Classification: LCC F1483.2 (ebook)
LCC F1483.2 .M38 2018 (print) | DDC 972.84–dc23
LC record available at https://lccn.loc.gov/2018018387

Editor: Kristine Spanier
Designer: Molly Ballanger

Photo Credits: Henryk Sadura/Shutterstock, cover;
John Coletti/Getty, 1; Pixfiction/Shutterstock, 3;
Matyas Rehak/Shutterstock, 4; Salvanatura/AP Images,
5; Matt Jeppson/Shutterstock, 6-7tl; Cynthia Kidwell/
Shutterstock, 6-7tr; My Lit'l Eye/Shutterstock, 6-7bl;
Matt9122/Shutterstock, 6-7br; John Mitchell/Alamy,
8-9, 20-21; Milosz Maslanka/Shutterstock, 10, 12-13;
Guayo Fuentes/Shutterstock, 11; US Congress/Alamy,
14-15; Photo Works/Shutterstock, 16; paul kennedy/
Alamy, 17; Anna_Pustynnikova/Shutterstock, 18-19;
Rose Possien/Le Vintique, 20-21r; YamabikaY/
Shutterstock, 23.

Printed in the United States of America at
Corporate Graphics in North Mankato, Minnesota.

TABLE OF CONTENTS

CHAPTER 1

WELCOME TO EL SALVADOR!

Hike around the **crater** of a volcano. Gaze at Mayan **ruins**. Visit a cloud forest. Welcome to El Salvador!

Santa Ana Volcano

This country has 23 active volcanoes. The tallest is Santa Ana. How tall is it? 7,812 feet (2,381 meters)!

boa constrictor

coati

turquoise-browed motmot

tiger shark

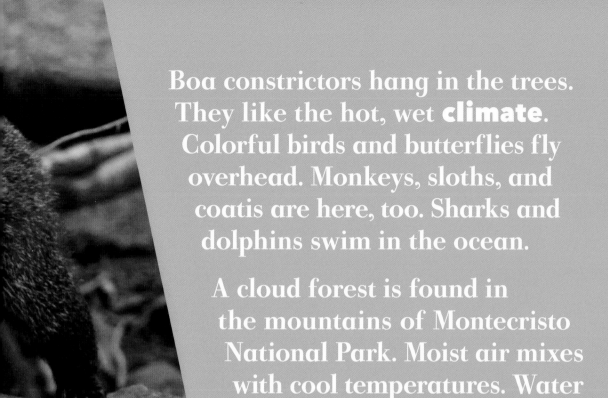

Boa constrictors hang in the trees. They like the hot, wet **climate**. Colorful birds and butterflies fly overhead. Monkeys, sloths, and coatis are here, too. Sharks and dolphins swim in the ocean.

A cloud forest is found in the mountains of Montecristo National Park. Moist air mixes with cool temperatures. Water **condenses**. It surrounds the forest in mist and fog.

DID YOU KNOW?

Giant oak and laurel trees are here. Some grow more than 90 feet (27 m) tall! The forest floor is covered in ferns, orchids, and moss.

Look at the beautiful murals in Ataco! Each one tells a story. About what? The **culture** of the country. Family life. History. Who paints them? Artists from the area.

WHAT DO YOU THINK?

Are there murals where you live? What kinds of stories do they tell? If you were to create a mural, what would you show?

mural

CHAPTER 2

LIFE IN EL SALVADOR

The land here was once part of the Mayan **Empire**. When? More than 3,000 years ago! Mayan people built **temples**. Visitors can still view them.

Now most people here live in cities. San Salvador has the biggest **population**. It is the **capital**. How many people live here? More than 1 million!

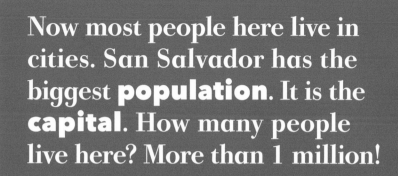

San Salvador

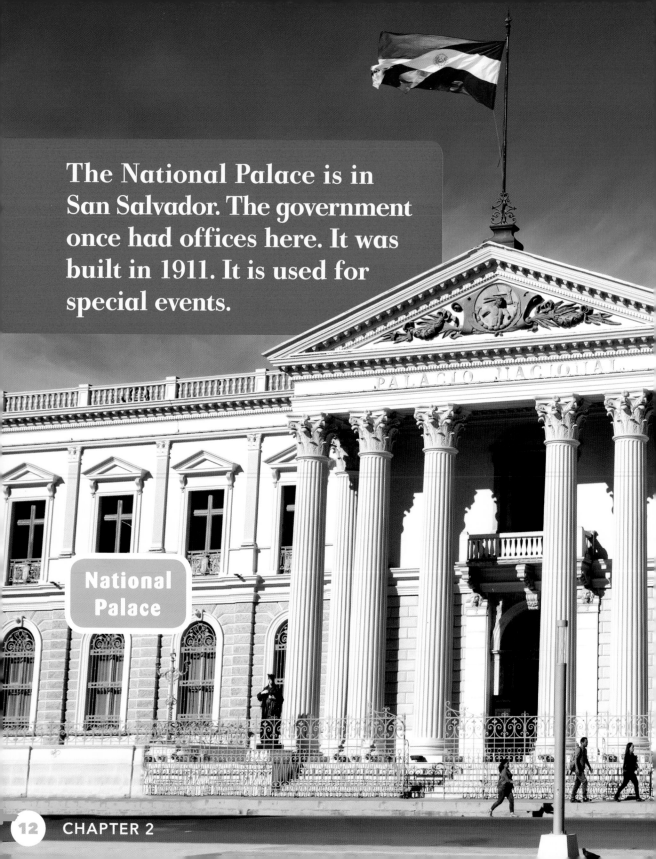

The National Palace is in San Salvador. The government once had offices here. It was built in 1911. It is used for special events.

National Palace

TAKE A LOOK!

Spain ruled El Salvador for hundreds of years. It took more than 300 years for the country to become fully **independent**.

1524
invaded by Spain

1823
becomes part of the United Provinces of Central America; includes Guatemala, Honduras, Nicaragua, and Costa Rica

1821
declares independence

1540
becomes a Spanish colony

1841
becomes fully independent

The government pays for children to attend school for nine years. They receive free uniforms and school supplies. If they want to go to high school, they must pay **tuition**. Some families cannot afford it.

Children may begin working on farms instead. What are the biggest **crops**? Coffee and sugarcane. Children help their families in other ways. They haul water home. They wash clothes. They may care for younger siblings.

CHAPTER 3
EL SALVADOR'S PEOPLE

Soccer is a favorite sport here. So is boxing.

People enjoy swimming in the ocean. Surfers ride the waves. Others might hike in the mountains.

What is for dinner? Tortillas filled with meat, beans, or cheese. Corn bread is eaten every day. So are beans. Fresh, tropical fruits are found all over the country. A popular dessert is tres leches cake. It is made with three different kinds of milk!

WHAT DO YOU THINK?

Families here usually eat the main meal of the day together. Do you eat meals with your family regularly? What are the benefits of families eating together?

tres leches
cake

Markets are filled with crafts made by people here. You may find hand-painted wood carvings. Or woven **textiles**. You may also find a table filled with "sorpresas," or surprises. These are miniature scenes and figures hidden inside of shells the size of an egg.

El Salvador is an interesting country. What would you want to see first?

sorpresa ·····▶

QUICK FACTS & TOOLS

EL SALVADOR

Location: Central America

Size: 8,124 square miles (21,041 square kilometers)

Population: 6,172,011 (July 2017 estimate)

Capital: San Salvador

Type of Government: presidential republic

Languages: Spanish and Nawat

Exports: clothing, coffee, sugar, chemicals

Currency: U.S. dollar

GLOSSARY

capital: A city where government leaders meet.

climate: The weather typical of a certain place over a long period of time.

condenses: When moisture in air forms tiny drops of water.

crater: The mouth of a volcano or geyser.

crops: Plants grown for food.

culture: The ideas, customs, traditions, and ways of life of a group of people.

empire: A group of countries or states that has the same ruler.

independent: Free from a controlling authority.

population: The total number of people who live in a place.

ruins: The remains of something that has collapsed or been destroyed.

temples: Buildings used for worship.

textiles: Woven or knitted fabrics or cloths.

tuition: Money paid to a school in order for a student to study there.

El Salvador's currency

INDEX

TO LEARN MORE

Learning more is as easy as 1, 2, 3.

1) Go to www.factsurfer.com

2) Enter "ElSalvador" into the search box.

3) Click the "Surf" button to see a list of websites.

With factsurfer, finding more information is just a click away.